Y0-BQN-610

New York Yankees Baseball

Progressive Trivia

Researched by Al Netzer

Paul F. Wilson & Tom P. Rippey III, Editors

Kick The Ball, Ltd

Lewis Center, Ohio

Progressive Trivia Books
by Kick The Ball, Ltd

Professional Baseball
Boston Red Sox
New York Yankees
St. Louis Cardinals

Professional Football
Pittsburgh Steelers

New York Yankees Baseball: Progressive Trivia;
First Edition 2012

Published by
Kick The Ball, Ltd
8595 Columbus Pike, Suite 197
Lewis Center, OH 43035
www.ProgressiveTriviaBooks.com

Edited by: Paul F. Wilson & Tom P. Rippey III
Designed and Formatted by Paul F. Wilson
Researched by: Al Netzer

Copyright © 2012 by Kick The Ball, Ltd, Lewis Center, Ohio

ALL RIGHTS RESERVED. No part of this book may be reproduced or transmitted in any form whatsoever, electronic, or mechanical, including photocopying, recording, or by any informational storage or retrieval system without the expressed written, dated and signed permission from the copyright holder.

Trademarks and Copyrights: Kick The Ball, Ltd is not associated with any event, team, conference, or league mentioned in this book. All trademarks are the property of their respective owners. Kick The Ball, Ltd respects and honors the copyrights and trademarks of others. We use event, team, conference, or league names only as points of reference in our books. Names, statistics, and others facts obtained through public domain resources.

LIMIT OF LIABILITY/DISCLAIMER OF WARRANTY: THE RESEARCHER AND PUBLISHER HAVE USED GREAT CARE IN RESEARCHING AND WRITING THIS BOOK. HOWEVER, WE MAKE NO REPRESENTATION OR WARRANTIES AS TO THE COMPLETENESS OF ITS CONTENTS OR THEIR ACCURACY AND WE SPECIFICALLY DISCLAIM ANY IMPLIED WARRANTIES OF MERCHANTABILITY OR FITNESS FOR A PARTICULAR PURPOSE. WARRANTIES MAY NOT BE CREATED OR EXTENDED BY ANY SALES MATERIALS OR SALESPERSON OF THIS BOOK. NEITHER THE RESEARCHER NOR THE PUBLISHER SHALL BE LIABLE FOR ANY LOSS OF PROFIT OR ANY OTHER COMMERCIAL DAMAGES, INCLUDING BUT NOT LIMITED TO SPECIAL, INCIDENTAL, CONSEQUENTIAL, OR OTHER DAMAGES.

For information on ordering this book in bulk at reduced prices, please email us at pfwilson@progressivetriviabooks.com.

International Standard Book Number: 978-1-61320-042-1

Printed and Bound in the United States of America

10 9 8 7 6 5 4 3 2 1

Table of Contents

Questions and Answers 1-180.............................. Page 1

Questions and Answers 181-360............................. Page 31

Questions and Answers 361-540.......................Page 61

Questions and Answers 541-720........................... Page 91

About
Progressive Trivia Books
by Kick The Ball, Ltd

Play **New York Yankees Baseball: Progressive Trivia** by yourself or with others, either way we hope you enjoy playing.

Each page of this book presents six questions that relate in some way to one another. Likewise, each question progresses through that page's theme in a way that builds on the previous question's answer, or the previous question itself. In so doing, a more complete picture emerges about the subject matter of that set of six questions.

Questions can take the form of: multiple choice; true or false; yes or no; fill in the blank; or simply a question with no answer options at all. Each type of question challenges you in a unique way to test your knowledge of the team's history, great moments, traditions, key players and coaches, championships, individual and team records, and much more.

The answers to each set of questions are conveniently placed at the bottom of that page. You may want to *cover the answers prior to beginning a section* to avoid prematurily revealing an answer to yourself.

Although we have taken care to avoid errors in this book, from time to time they may occur. If you find one, we ask for your understanding and thank you for bringing it to our attention. Please email tprippey@progressivetriviabooks.com with any comments or observations. Thank you and we sincerely hope you enjoy playing **New York Yankees Baseball: Progressive Trivia.**

All information in this book is valid
as of the end of the
2011 season.

New York Yankees Baseball

1) Who is the Yankees' all-time games pitched leader?

2) How many total games pitched did he have?

3) When did he break New York's previous record?

4) Where did he set the record?

   A) Boston
   B) Chicago
   C) Oakland
   D) New York

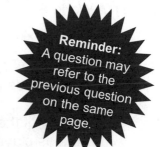

Reminder: A question may refer to the previous question on the same page.

5) What years did he play for the Yankees?

6) What year did the Yankees sign him?

Answers:

1) Mariano Rivera
2) 1,042
3) April 27, 2004
4) D – New York
5) 1995-present
6) 1990

Progressive Trivia

7) Who was the Yankees' most recent World Series MVP?

8) How many times have Yankees players been named World Series MVP?

9) A World Series MVP award was first given to a Yankee in
_____.

10) Where does New York rank in its all-time number of World Series MVPs compared to other MLB teams?

11) In which of their World Series appearances did a Yankees player not win the MVP award (since 1955)?

12) Reggie Jackson had five home runs in route to winning a World Series MVP award against which team?

Answers:

7) Hideki Matsui
8) 12
9) 1956
10) First; The LA Dodgers are next with seven.
11) 1955, 1957, 1963, 1964, 1976, 1981, 2001 and 2003
12) Los Angeles Dodgers

☆ **rogressive Tr ia** ☆

13) When was the ground breaking for Yankee Stadium III?

14) What was the stadium's cost of construction?

15) What is the stadium's seating capacity?

16) Who owns the stadium?

17) Who is the Yankees' co-tenant at the stadium?

18) The stadium's playing surface is artificial turf.

    A) True
    B) False

Answers:

13) Aug. 19, 2006
14) $1.5 billion
15) 50,287
16) New York Yankees
17) Pinstripe Bowl; An NCAA college football bowl
18) B – False; Kentucky Bluegrass

☆ Progressive Trivia ☆

19) What was the original name of the New York Yankees?

20) _____ bought the franchise and moved it to New York.

21) Did the team play its first-ever game in 1882?

    A) Yes
    B) No

22) The team's name was officially changed to the New York Yankees in what year?

23) What was the name of the team's first home park?

24) To which league did the team originally belong?

    A) American Association
    B) Union Association
    C) American League
    D) Federal League

Answers:

19) New York Highlanders
20) Bill Devery and Frank Farrell
21) B – No; 1903
22) 1913
23) Hilltop Park
24) C – American League

25) What year did pinstripes first appear on Yankees uniforms?

26) The Yankees interlocking "NY" logo appears on their away uniforms.

    A) True
    B) False

27) Which team insignia currently appears on both home and away team caps?

28) The Yankees home uniform has remained unchanged since what year?

29) What color is the Yankees' current road uniform?

30) What color is the interlocking "NY" logo?

Answers:

25) 1912
26) B – False; "NEW YORK"
27) Interlocking "NY"
28) 1936; The longest in the Major Leagues.
29) Gray
30) Midnight Blue

31) There are more than 20 New York Yankees players, coaches, contributors and administrators enshrined in the National Baseball Hall of Fame.

    A) True
    B) False

32) What year was the first Yankee enshrined into the National Baseball Hall of Fame?

33) How many Yankees were members of the National Baseball Hall of Fame's 1974 class?

34) Which of the following positions are represented the most by Yankees in the NBHoF?

    A) Center Field
    B) Pitcher
    C) Second Base
    D) Right Field

35) Casey Stengel was a member of which class?

36) What distinction does Lou Gehrig hold in the NBHoF?

Answers:

31) A – True; 23
32) 1936
33) Two; Whitey Ford and Mickey Mantle
34) B – Pitcher; Seven selections
35) 1966
36) First-ever player to have his uniform number retired

37) How many draft picks did the Yankees have in the 2011 MLB First-Year Player Draft?

38) Who did New York select with their only selection on the first day of the 2011 draft?

39) The Yankees 2011 second-round draft pick was a player from which university?

    A) Arizona State
    B) Texas
    C) Western Kentucky
    D) Rice

40) All time, how many players have the Yankees drafted out of Texas?

41) Who was the first-ever player the Yankees drafted from Texas?

42) What year did New York draft its first-ever player from Texas?

Answers:

37) 50
38) Dante Bichette, Jr.; A compensation pick
39) B – Texas
40) 17
41) David Brown
42) 1969; Two players that year

43) The Yankees have made _____ all-time appearances in the World Series?

44) Which MLB club has New York played the most in the Fall Classic?

45) What is the Yankees' all-time record in the World Series?

46) Did the Yankees travel to Miami, Fla. for games in their most recent World Series appearance?

    A) Yes
    B) No

47) What is the Yankees' all-time winning percentage in the World Series?

48) How many World Series titles has the Yankees franchise won?

Answers:

43) 40
44) Los Angeles Dodgers; 11 times
45) 134-90
46) B – No; Philadelphia, Pa.
47) .675
48) 27

49) Mariano Rivera is the Yankees' all-time Earned Run Average (ERA) leader (minimum 750.0 innings pitched).

   A) True
   B) False

50) What is his career ERA?

51) How many seasons has he played in New York?

52) Who is second on the all-time career ERA leaders list, Russ Ford or Jack Chesbro?

53) What is the ERA of the No. 2 player on the list?

54) Besides Rivera, do any other current Yankees rank in the top five of the team's all-time ERA leaders list?

   A) Yes
   B) No

Answers:

49) A – True
50) 2.21
51) 17
52) Russ Ford
53) 2.54
54) B – No

55) Whose jersey number was the first-ever retired by the New York Yankees?

56) What year was his jersey number officially retired?

57) What was his uniform number?

58) How many total uniform numbers has the Yankees organization officially retired?

59) What jersey number has been retired twice by the team?

60) Whose jersey number was the most recent to be retired by the Yankees organization?

Answers:

55) Lou Gehrig
56) 1940
57) No. 4
58) 15
59) No. 8; Yogi Berra and Bill Dickey
60) Ron Guidry; No. 49

61) In 2000, which club won the NLCS to earn a trip to the Fall Classic to face the New York Yankees?

62) Game 5 of the 2000 World Series was played in the city of _____.

63) What is the name of the ballpark in which the game was played?

64) How many games did the Yankees win in the series?

65) Who was the 2000 World Series MVP?

66) Who was the Yankees' skipper at the time?

Answers:

61) New York Mets
62) Flushing, N.Y.
63) Shea Stadium
64) Four
65) Derek Jeter
66) Joe Torre

☆ **Progressive Trivia** ☆

67) Who owns the Yankees' individual record for the most career home runs?

68) How many home runs did he hit as a Yankee?

    A) 659
    B) 671
    C) 703
    D) 714

69) How many seasons did he play for the Yankees?

70) When was his first season with the team?

71) How many games did he pitch for the Yankees?

72) What was his real name?

Answers:

67) Babe Ruth
68) A – 659
69) 15
70) 1920
71) Five; Winning all five
72) George Herman Ruth

☆ **Progressive Trivia** ☆

73) When was the Yankees' record for the longest home run hit in Yankee Stadium I set?

74) Who is credited with that home run?

75) How many feet was the record-setting home run?

76) Against which club was the record set?

    A) Detroit Tigers
    B) Washington Senators
    C) Chicago White Sox
    D) Kansas City Athletics

77) Was the home run hit off the Athletics' Orlando Pena?

    A) Yes
    B) No

78) How many runs were scored on the hit?

Answers:

73) May 22, 1963
74) Mickey Mantle
75) 620; This is an estimated distance as the ball hit a
    façade in right field 110 feet above the stadium.
76) D – Kansas City Athletics
77) B – No; Bill Fischer
78) One; It was a walk-off home run in the 11th inning.

New York Yankees Baseball

79) Who holds the Yankees' pitching record for the most wins in a single season?

80) When did he set the team record in the category?

81) How many decisions did he win that season?

82) How many losses did he record that season?

83) Did he throw right- or left-handed?

84) The second highest number of wins he recorded in a single season was 28.

   A) True
   B) False

Answers:

79) Jack Chesbro
80) 1904
81) 41
82) 12
83) Right
84) A – True; In 1902 with the Pittsburgh Pirates

85) The Yankees' record for the most career shutouts thrown is owned by which pitcher?

    A) Mel Stottlemyre
    B) Ron Guidry
    C) Red Ruffing
    D) Whitey Ford

86) How many career shutouts did he toss?

87) How many seasons did it take to accumulate his record-setting number of career shutouts?

88) How many years did he spend with the Yankees?

89) His career total in the category is twice as high as the next highest Yankees pitcher on the list.

    A) True
    B) False

90) Does he also own the team record for the most shutouts thrown in a single season?

Answers:

85) D – Whitey Ford
86) 45
87) 16
88) 16
89) B – False; M. Stottlemyre and R. Ruffing each had 40.
90) No

91) What is the Yankees' record for the most singles hit by a batter in a single game?

92) Who originally set the record?

93) Against what team was the record set?

94) What year did he set the team record?

95) How many RBIs resulted from his singles that game?

   A) 1
   B) 4
   C) 6
   D) 8

96) Does he also own the Yankees' record for the most singles hit in a single season?

Answers:

91) Six
92) Myril Hoag; Matched by Johnny Damon in 2008
93) Boston Red Sox
94) 1934
95) A – 1
96) No

97) Mickey Mantle holds the Yankees' career record for the most runs batted in (RBIs).

    A) True
    B) False

98) How many RBIs does the career leader have?

99) When was his first season with the team?

100) When was his final season with the team?

101) How many RBIs did Babe Ruth have during his career in New York?

102) Who is third on the Yankees' list for the category and how many RBIs did he have?

Answers:

97) B – False; Lou Gehrig
98) 1,995
99) 1923
100) 1939
101) 1,971
102) Joe DiMaggio, 1,537

☆ **Progressive Trivia** ☆

103) Who was the Yankees' opponent in the 2009 World Series?

104) Which team did the Yankees defeat in the ALCS to advance to the World Series?

105) The Yankees defeated their 2009 World Series opponent with a series record of four games to two.

A) True
B) False

106) How many total runs did the Yankees score in the 2009 World Series?

107) Did New York have home field advantage for the series?

108) Which Yankees pitcher closed out the final inning of the series?

Answers:

103) Philadelphia Phillies
104) Los Angeles Angels
105) A – True
106) 32
107) Yes
108) Mariano Rivera

☆ **Progressive Trivia** ☆

109) What are the most putouts by a Yankee in a single game?

110) Who was the last to tie the Yankees' record for the most putouts in a game?

111) When did he tie the team record in the category?

112) Against which team was the record tied?

113) When was the original record for the most putouts by a Yankee in a single game set?

114) Who originally set the record for most putouts by a Yankee in a single game?

    A) Kid Elberfeld
    B) Wid Conroy
    C) Hal Chase
    D) Jimmy Williams

Answers:

109) 22
110) Don Mattingly
111) July 20, 1987
112) Minnesota Twins
113) 1906
114) C – Hal Chase

115) The Yankees' team record for the most hits in a single game was set versus the Boston Red Sox.

    A) True
    B) False

116) How many total hits did the team have that day?

117) When was the record in the category set?

118) How many runs resulted from the team's hits that day?

119) Were any of the hits a home run?

120) Did the Yankees win the ball game as a result of the team's record-setting performance?

Answers:

115) A – True
116) 30
117) Sept. 28, 1923
118) 24
119) Yes; Two
120) Yes; Yankees 24, Red Sox 4

New York Yankees Baseball

121) Who holds the Yankees' record for the most walks in a single season?

    A) Babe Ruth
    B) Lou Gehrig
    C) Derek Jeter
    D) Bernie Williams

122) How many walks did he have to set the team record?

123) What year did he have his record-setting performance?

124) He led the team 11 seasons in the category during his career.

    A) True
    B) False

125) Mickey Mantle had ___ walks in 1957.

126) What spot does Mickey Mantle hold on the Yankees' leaders list?

Answers:

121) A – Babe Ruth
122) 170
123) 1923
124) A – True
125) 140
126) Third

127) What are the most games the Yankees have ever won in a single season?

128) What year did the Yankees win the most games in franchise history?

129) Did the Yankees win 10 straight games from June 30 to July 12?

130) Which club ended the Yankees' record consecutive wins streak?

131) Did the 2011 Yankees win eight consecutive games?

132) Which team did the Yankees defeat to begin their longest win streak of 2011?

Answers:

127) 114
128) 1998
129) Yes
130) Cleveland Indians
131) Yes
132) Baltimore Orioles

133) _____ was the most recent player to tie the Yankees' record for the most runs scored in a single game.

134) What season did he tie this mark?

135) Against which team did he score the record-tying runs?

136) Was the record tied at home or away?

137) How many at-bats did he have during the game?

138) How many runs did he score that day?

Answers:

133) Johnny Damon
134) 2006
135) Toronto Blue Jays
136) Home
137) Five
138) Five; This has been done 16 times by a Yankee.

139) What is the Yankees' team record for the most errors committed in a single game?

140) Against which opponent were the errors committed?

141) What season did this occur?

142) Did the Yankees win the game despite their team errors?

143) That year, the Yankees also went on to set a team record for the most errors committed in a season.

    A) True
    B) False

144) Which season was the team record for the most errors committed set?

Answers:

139) 10
140) Detroit Tigers
141) 1907
142) No
143) B – False
144) 1912; 386 errors

145) What year was George Steinbrenner III born?

146) Where was he born?

147) What year did he purchase the Yankees franchise?

148) How much did he pay for the team?

    A) $5 million
    B) $7.3 million
    C) $8.7 million
    D) $10 million

149) What was Steinbrenner's nickname?

150) His tenure of ownership was the longest in franchise history.

    A) True
    B) False

Answers:

145) 1930
146) Rocky River, Ohio
147) 1973
148) C – $8.7 million
149) The Boss
150) A – True; 37 years, 13 more than any other owner

151) Which Yankee holds the team's record for the most career runs scored?

152) How many career runs did he score?

153) His last season in a Yankees uniform was in _____.

154) How many career hits did he record?

155) How many career plate appearances did he have?

156) He was selected to the All-Star game 12 times while playing for the Yankees.

    A) True
    B) False

Answers:

151) Babe Ruth
152) 1,959
153) 1934
154) 2,518
155) 9,198
156) B – False; He was selected to the first two All-Star games, 1933 and 1934.

157) The Yankees' career record for the most games started is held by _____.

158) How many total career games did he start?

159) He was a Yankee from 1950 through which season?

    A) 1961
    B) 1964
    C) 1967
    D) 1970

160) Were his career total games started greater than Andy Pettitte's and Red Ruffing's combined?

161) Who is ranked second on the career leaders list for this category?

162) How many total career games started does the No. 2 player on the list have?

Answers:

157) Whitey Ford
158) 438
159) C – 1967
160) No
161) Andy Pettitte
162) 396

163) Where did the Yankees set the team record for the most runs scored in a game?

    A) Home
    B) Away

164) What team played the Yankees that day?

165) Was the game played before or after the All-Star break?

166) Which team had the better record heading into the game?

167) How many runs did the Yankees score in the first inning?

168) What was the final score of the game?

Answers:

163) B – Away
164) Philadelphia Athletics
165) Before
166) New York Yankees
167) Zero
168) Yankees 25, Athletics 2

★ Progressive Trivia ★

169) Who holds the Yankees' record for the most hits
     allowed by a pitcher in a game?

    A) Mel Stottlemyre
    B) Red Ruffing
    C) Lefty Gomez
    D) Jack Quinn

170) Who was the opposing team in that game?

171) How many hits did they record?

172) How many runs did the opposing team score that
     day?

173) Did the Yankees lose the game?

174) Did this pitcher spend his entire career with the
     Yankees?

    A) Yes
    B) No

Answers:

169) D – Jack Quinn
170) Boston Red Sox
171) 21
172) 13
173) Yes
174) B – No; Eight teams in 23 years

★ **Progressive Trivia** ★

175) The Yankees' career record for the most at-bats by a
player is over 10,000.

A) True
B) False

176) Who holds the team record in the category?

177) When was his first year with the Yankees?

178) Has he ever led the league in at-bats in a season?

179) Does he also hold the MLB record for the category?

180) Who is ranked second on the Yankees' career leaders
list for this category?

Answers:

175) B – False; 9,868
176) Derek Jeter
177) 1995
178) No
179) No
180) Mickey Mantle

181) All time, how many times have Yankees been selected to the MLB All-Star Game?

182) How many Yankees were selected to the All-Star Game in 1933, the inaugural MLB All-Star Game?

183) What is the highest number of Yankees to be selected to the All-Star Game in a year?

184) What year were the most Yankees selected for the game?

185) Since 1933, how many times was only one Yankee selected for the All-Star Game in a year?

186) Who holds the Yankees' record for the most selections to the All-Star Game?

Answers:

181) 399
182) Six
183) 11
184) 1939
185) Five
186) Mickey Mantle; 20

☆ **Progressive Trivia** ☆

187) When was the longest game played, by number of innings, in New York Yankees history?

    A) May 24, 1918
    B) Aug. 21, 1933
    C) June 24, 1962
    D) June 1, 2003

188) How many innings were played that game?

189) Who was the Yankees' opponent that game?

190) How many hours did the game last?

191) What was the final score of the contest?

192) What is the second longest game played, by number of innings played in team history?

Answers:

187) C – June 24, 1962
188) 22
189) Detroit Tigers
190) Seven
191) Yankees 9, Tigers 7
192) 20 innings

193) Did Earl Combs hit more triples in his career as a Yankee than Lou Gehrig?

194) Who hit the third most career triples in Yankees history?

195) How many triples did he hit?

196) How many seasons was he in New York?

197) How many total triples did Lou Gehrig hit in his MLB career?

198) Does Lou Gehrig also hold the MLB record for the most triples hit by a player in a career?

Answers:

193) No; Gehrig hit nine more than Combs.
194) Joe DiMaggio
195) 131
196) 13
197) 163
198) No

199) What is New York's team record for the most runs allowed in a single game?

200) Which opponent accomplished this feat?

201) Where was this game played?

    A) Home
    B) Away

202) What is New York's team record for the second most runs allowed?

203) Which team holds this record?

204) Where was this game played?

    A) Home
    B) Away

Answers:

199) 24
200) Cleveland Indians
201) B – Away
202) 22
203) Cleveland Indians
204) A – Home

205) Who was the Yankees' opponent in the 2003 World Series?

206) Where was Game 3 of the series played?

207) What is the name of the stadium in which Game 3 was played?

208) Did the Yankees ever lead the series?

209) Was a Game 7 played that series?

210) Who won the series?

Answers:

205) Florida Marlins
206) Miami, Fla.
207) Pro Player Stadium
208) Yes
209) No
210) Florida Marlins

211) _____ holds the Yankees' record for the most home runs in a season.

212) What year did he set the team record for the category?

213) How many home runs did he have that season?

214) Who holds the No. 2 spot on the list for the category?

215) How many home runs did the No. 2 player hit in a season to earn his place on the list?

216) What year was the No. 2 spot secured?

     A) 1921
     B) 1927
     C) 1928
     D) 1931

Answers:

211) Roger Maris
212) 1961
213) 61
214) Babe Ruth
215) 60
216) B – 1927

217) Who was the first-ever Yankee to become the AL Batting Champion?

218) What year did he win the title?

219) What was his batting average that season?

220) Who was the most recent Yankee to become the AL Batting Champion?

221) All time, how many Yankees have been named the AL batting champion?

    A) 5
    B) 8
    C) 10
    D) 11

222) Which Yankee earned the title the most times?

Answers:

217) Babe Ruth
218) 1924
219) .378
220) Bernie Williams
221) B – 8
222) Joe DiMaggio; Twice

223) Who owns the Yankees' record for the most career putouts?

224) How many career putouts did he have?

225) He played for the Yankees from 1923-_____.

226) Does Wally Pipp have 10,000 fewer putouts than Lou Gehrig?

227) How many career putouts does Wally Pipp have?

228) How many seasons did it take him to accumulate his second-best number of putouts?

Answers:

223) Lou Gehrig
224) 19,540
225) 1939
226) No
227) 15,171
228) 11

229) Fritz Maisel holds the Yankees' record for the most stolen bases by a player in a season.

    A) True
    B) False

230) What is the Yankees' record for the most stolen bases by a player in a season?

231) When was the record set?

232) How many times does Rickey Henderson appear in the top 10 spots of this category?

233) Who holds the No. 2 spot on the list?

234) He had _____ stolen bases in the _____ season.

Answers:

229) B – False; Rickey Henderson
230) 93
231) 1988
232) Three
233) Rickey Henderson
234) 87, 1986

235) What is the Yankees' pitching record for the most
bases on balls in a single game?

236) Who holds the record?

237) Against what team was the record set?

238) What year was the record set?

239) Lefty Gomez holds the Yankees' single-season
pitching record for the most bases on balls.

A) True
B) False

240) Who holds the Yankees' record for the second most
bases on balls by a pitcher in a season?

Answers:

235) 13
236) Tommy Byrne
237) Detroit Tigers
238) 1949
239) B – False; Tommy Byrne, 179
240) Bob Turley; 177

241) Joe Girardi is a graduate of which university?

242) How many seasons did Girardi play for the Yankees?

243) What season did Girardi rejoin the Yankees as their manager?

244) Has he served as a manager for any other MLB franchise?

245) What position did he play as an MLB player?

246) What year was he named NL Manager of the Year.

Answers:

241) Northwestern University
242) Four; 1996-99
243) 2008
244) Yes; Florida Marlins
245) Catcher
246) 2006

247) Who was the first-ever Yankee to receive the Rolaids Relief Man Award?

248) What year did he receive the award?

249) How many times did he receive the award?

250) All time, how many Yankees relievers have received the award?

251) Who was the most recent Yankee to receive the honor?

252) What year did he receive the honor?

Answers:

247) Rich "Goose" Gossage
248) 1978
249) Once
250) Four; A total of nine times
251) Mariano Rivera
252) 2009

253) All time, how many team captains have the Yankees had?

254) Who was the first-ever captain of the Yankees?

255) What year was he named Yankees captain?

256) Who, along with Ron Guidry, was named co-captain in 1986?

257) Babe Ruth was a Yankee captain for only five days.

    A) True
    B) False

258) Who is the current captain of the Yankees?

Answers:

253) 11
254) Hal Chase
255) 1912
256) Willie Randolph
257) A – True
258) Derek Jeter

259) The Yankee with the highest career batting average was traded to New York from which team?

260) Who holds the record?

261) What was his career batting average?

262) Who is second on the career list in the category?

263) What was his career batting average?

264) What was his career batting average in MLB?

Answers:

259) Boston Red Sox
260) Babe Ruth
261) .349
262) Lou Gehrig
263) .340
264) .342

265) How many Yankees pitchers have thrown a no-hitter?

266) Which of the following Yankees pitchers did not throw a no-hitter?

    A) Sad Sam Jones
    B) Jim Abbott
    C) Whitey Ford
    D) Dave Righetti

267) Who was the first-ever Yankee to toss a no-hitter?

268) What year and against which team did he accomplish the feat?

269) Who is the most recent Yankee to throw a no-no?

270) What year and against which team did he accomplish the feat?

Answers:

265) 10
266) C – Whitey Ford
267) George Mogridge
268) 1917, Boston Red Sox
269) David Cone
270) 1999, Montreal Expos

271) Wally Pipp owns the Yankees' record for the most putouts in a single season.

   A) True
   B) False

272) How many putouts did he have in a single season?

273) What season was the record set?

274) How many games did he play in that season?

275) _____ had the second most putouts that season.

276) How many putouts did he have that season?

Answers:

271) A – True
272) 1,667
273) 1922
274) 152
275) Wally Schang
276) 456

277) What decade did the Yankees have their highest winning percentage?

278) What was their winning percentage that decade?

279) How many World Series Championships did they win that decade?

280) What decade did the Yankees have their lowest winning percentage?

281) What was their winning percentage that decade?

282) How many World Series Championships did they win that decade?

Answers:

277) 1930s
278) .636
279) Five
280) 1910s
281) .475
282) None

283) A Yankees batter has hit two grand slams in a single game.

    A) True
    B) False

284) Who accomplished that feat?

285) Against which team did he do it?

286) Did the Yankees win that contest?

287) Against which team did a Yankee hit a grand slam on his birthday?

288) Who accomplished that feat?

Answers:

283) A – True
284) Tony Lazzeri
285) Philadelphia Athletics
286) Yes
287) Oakland Athletics
288) Hideki Matsui

289) Who holds the Yankees' record for the most consecutive games hitting a home run?

290) How many consecutive games did he hit a home run during the streak?

291) What season did he set that mark?

292) Against what team did the streak begin?

293) Did he have two or more HRs in any of those games?

294) Against which team did the streak end?

Answers:

289) Don Mattingly
290) Eight
291) 1987
292) Minnesota Twins
293) Yes; He hit two home runs in two of the eight games.
294) Texas Rangers

295) Who was New York's first-ever batting Triple Crown winner?

296) What year did he win the Triple Crown?

297) Who was the most recent Yankee to win the batting Triple Crown?

298) What year did he win the Triple Crown?

299) All time, how many times has a Yankees player won the batting Triple Crown?

300) Has a Yankees player ever won the pitching Triple Crown?

Answers:

295) Lou Gehrig
296) 1934
297) Mickey Mantle
298) 1956
299) Two
300) Yes; Lefty Gomez in 1934 and 1937

301) What was given the nickname of "Murderers' Row"?

302) What year was the nickname popularized?

303) Earle Combs, Babe Ruth, Lou Gehrig, Mark Koenig, Bob Meusel and Tony Lazzeri were all notable members of Murderers' Row?

   A) True
   B) False

304) Which Yankees batter had 231 hits that season?

305) What was the Yankees' regular-season record that year?

306) How many members of Murderers' Row are in the National Baseball Hall of Fame?

Answers:

301) The first six batters in the Yankee lineup.
302) 1927
303) A – True
304) Earle Combs
305) 110-44
306) Four; E. Combs, B. Ruth, L. Gehrig and T. Lazzeri

307) Who holds the Yankees' record for the most career plate appearances?

308) How many career plate appearances does he have?

309) He accumulated his team-leading plate appearances from _____ to _____.

310) How many times was he named a Gold Glove Award winner?

311) How many times was he named a Silver Slugger?

312) He is a 12-time All-Star selection.

    A) True
    B) False

Answers:

307) Derek Jeter
308) 11,155
309) 1995, 2011; Still active
310) Five; 2004, 2005, 2006, 2009 and 2010
311) Four; 2006, 2007, 2008 and 2009
312) A – True

313) Joe Girardi is the _____ all-time manager of the New York Yankees.

314) What year did Girardi take the helm as manager?

315) How old was he when he was hired as the Yankees' skipper?

316) Joe Girardi is the youngest-ever manager of the Yankees.

    A) True
    B) False

317) Where did Girardi end his playing career?

318) After Spring Training in 2004, what was Girardi's first job?

Answers:

313) 32nd
314) 2008
315) 43
316) B – False
317) St. Louis Cardinals
318) Commentator for YES Network

319) Has a Yankees fielder ever recorded an unassisted triple play?

320) Who recorded an unassisted triple play versus the Yankees?

321) What team did he play for?

322) What year did this occur?

323) Who hit a line drive to Velarde to start the unassisted triple play?

324) Did the Yankees win the game?

Answers:

319) No
320) Randy Velarde; The only one recorded against the Yankees.
321) Oakland Athletics
322) 2000
323) Shane Spencer
324) Yes; Athletics 1, Yankees 4

☆ **Progressive Trivia** ☆

325) The Yankees played the _____ in the 1999 World Series.

326) Were the Yankees held scoreless in any of the games?

327) How many games did the Yankees win?

328) Who was the series MVP?

329) Who did New York defeat in the ALCS to advance to the Fall Classic that year?

330) How many games were played in the ALCS that year?

Answers:

325) Atlanta Braves
326) No
327) Four; The Yankees swept the series.
328) Mariano Rivera
329) Boston Red Sox
330) Five

331) Who holds the Yankees' pitching record for the most strikeouts in a game?

    A) Ron Guidry
    B) David Cone
    C) CC Sabathia
    D) Jack Chesbro

332) How many strikeouts did he throw to set the team record?

333) What year was the record set?

334) Against which team was the record set?

335) How many times did Guidry retire the side in order during the game?

336) Is his team record also an MLB record?

Answers:

331) A – Ron Guidry
332) 18
333) 1978
334) California Angels
335) Four
336) No

337) How many Yankees were named to MLB's All-Century Team in 1999?

338) A fan vote and special panel selected the All-Century Team.

   A) True
   B) False

339) How many total players were listed on the All-Century Team ballot?

340) How many players were named to the starting line-up?

341) Which Yankee received the most overall votes?

342) Was Yogi Berra voted to the team by fans or added by the special blue ribbon panel?

Answers:

337) Six
338) A – True
339) 100
340) 30
341) Lou Gehrig; He led all players with 1,207,992 votes.
342) Voted to the team by fans

Progressive Trivia

343) Has a Yankees player ever won the Associated Press Athlete of the Year Award?

344) Roger Maris was the first-ever Yankee to win the Award.

    A) True
    B) False

345) Who was the first-ever Yankee to win the award?

346) What year was he honored with the award?

347) Who is the most recent Yankee to earn the distinction?

348) What year did he win the award?

Answers:

343) Yes
344) B – False
345) Joe DiMaggio
346) 1941
347) Ron Guidry
348) 1978

349) The Yankees' record for the most singles hit in a career is _____.

350) Who owns the team record in the category?

351) How many seasons has he played in New York?

352) Who holds the No. 2 spot in the category?

353) How many career singles did he hit?

354) Did he play more or fewer seasons in New York than the Yankee with the most career singles?

Answers:

349) 2,291
350) Derek Jeter
351) 17
352) Bernie Williams
353) 1,545
354) Fewer; 16 seasons

☆ **Progressive Trivia** ☆

355) All time, how many cycle hitters have the Yankees had?

356) How many of them were for the natural cycle?

357) Who was the first-ever Yankees batter to hit for the cycle?

358) Who was the only Yankees batter to hit for the natural cycle?

359) Who was the most recent Yankee to hit for the cycle?

360) Which Yankee hit for the cycle the most times?

Answers:

355) 11 players, 15 cycles
356) One
357) Bert Daniels; 1912
358) Tony Lazzeri; 1932
359) Melky Cabrera; 2009
360) Bob Meusel; Three times

Progressive Trivia

361) Since 1903, how many Yankees pitchers have recorded a grand slam?

362) Don Larsen recorded two grand slams in his career in New York.

    A) True
    B) False

363) Who was the most recent Yankee to give up a grand slam to a pitcher?

364) Has any Yankees pitcher hit more than two grand slams in his career?

365) Who is the most recent Yankees pitcher to hit a grand slam?

366) Against which team and pitcher did he hit it?

Answers:

361) Four
362) B – False
363) Al Downing; 1968
364) No
365) Mel Stottlemyre, 1965
366) Boston Red Sox, Bill Monbouquette

367) What season did the Yankees set the franchise record for most home runs allowed?

368) How many home runs did they allow?

369) Who gave up the most home runs that year?

370) Did the Yankees hit more home runs than they allowed that season?

371) What year did the Yankees give up the fewest home runs?

372) Did the Yankees hit more home runs than they allowed that season?

Answers:

367) 2004
368) 182
369) Javier Vazquez
370) Yes; 242
371) 1907; 13
372) Yes; 15

373) Was Game 1 of the 1998 World Series played at Yankee Stadium II?

374) Who was the Yankees' opponent in the 1998 World Series?

375) Who was the Yankees' starting pitcher for Game 1?

376) How did the Yankees score their first run of the series?

    A) Error
    B) Home Run
    C) RBI Double
    D) Sacrifice Fly

377) Who was named MVP of the World Series that year?

378) Derek Jeter had _____ total hits during the series.

Answers:

373) Yes
374) San Diego Padres
375) David Wells
376) C – RBI Double
377) Scott Brosius
378) Six

379) Mickey mantle had 2,000 strikeouts during his career in New York.

  A) True
  B) False

380) Were his strikeouts enough to set the Yankees' record for the category?

381) Who holds the No. 2 spot on the Yankees' career list in the category?

382) How many strikeouts does he have?

383) Yankees batters had _____ strikeouts during the 2011 season.

384) What spot does Babe Ruth hold on the Yankees' career list in the category?

Answers:

379) B – False; He had 1,710
380) Yes
381) Derek Jeter
382) 1,653
383) 1,138
384) No. 5; 1,122

Progressive Trivia

385) What year was the Yankees' team record for the highest batting average set?

386) What was their team batting average that year?

387) How many total team at-bats did the Yankees have that year?

388) The club also set their team record for the most at-bats that year?

    A) True
    B) False

389) How many total team plate appearances did the Yankees have that year?

390) Did the team set its record for the most plate appearances that year?

Answers:

385) 1930
386) .309
387) 5,448
388) B – False
389) 6,271
390) No

391) What are the most career saves by a Yankees pitcher at Yankee Stadium III?

392) Who holds the career saves record at Yankee Stadium III?

393) What are the second most saves by a Yankees pitcher at Yankee Stadium III?

394) Who holds that No. 2 spot in the category?

395) What are the third most saves by a Yankees pitcher at Yankee Stadium III?

396) Who holds that No. 3 spot in the category?

Answers:

391) 61
392) Mariano Rivera
393) 3
394) Joba Chamberlain
395) 2
396) Phil Coke and Alfredo Aceves

397) Who holds the Yankees' record for the most wild
pitches in a season?

A) Tim Leary
B) Ralph Terry
C) Bob Turley
D) A. J. Burnett

398) What year did he set the team record for the
category?

399) How many wild pitches did he throw?

400) Who is second on the Yankees' single-season list for
the category?

401) How many wild pitches did the No. 2 player throw?

402) What year did he secure the No. 2 spot on the list?

Answers:

397) D – A. J. Burnett
398) 2011
399) 25
400) Tim Leary
401) 23
402) 1990

403) "Already Home" by Jay-Z was an Alex Rodriguez walk-up song in 2011.

 A) True
 B) False

404) What was Mark Teixeira's walk-up song in 2011?

405) Did Nick Swisher select Mann featuring 50 Cent "Buzzin'" as his walk-up song in 2011?

406) What Jason Aldean song did Brett Gardener select as his walk-up song in 2011?

407) Which Yankee selected Enrique Iglesias' "Tonight I'm Loving You" as his walk-up song in 2011?

408) Yankees fans would expect to see _____ heading toward the pitchers mound when hearing Metallica's "Enter Sandman."

Answers:

403) A – True
404) "Bad Medicine" by Bon Jovi
405) Yes
406) "Dirt Road Anthem"
407) Robinson Cano
408) Mariano Rivera

409) Who was the first-ever black player to play for the Yankees?

410) What year did he first play for the team?

411) He was just one of two black players in MLB that season.

    A) True
    B) False

412) How many games did he play for New York?

413) How many seasons did he play in the major leagues?

414) Where did he end his career?

Answers:

409) Elston Howard
410) 1955
411) B – False
412) 1,492
413) 14
414) Boston Red Sox

415) What is the Yankees' team record for the most total bases in a game?

416) The record was set against the _____.

417) When was the record set?

418) Was the record set at home or away?

419) How many home runs did the Yankees have that game?

420) Who won the game?

Answers:

415) 53
416) Philadelphia Athletics
417) June 28, 1939
418) Away
419) Eight; This is a team record.
420) Yankees; Yankees 23, Athletics 2

421) Is the Yankees' team record for the highest fielding average in a season higher than .975?

422) What year was the team record set?

423) How many games did the team win that season?

    A) 89
    B) 95
    C) 101
    D) 103

424) Is the Yankees' team record for the lowest fielding average in a season below .900?

425) What year was that team record set?

426) How many games did the team win that season?

Answers:

421) Yes; .988
422) 2010
423) B – 95
424) No; .939
425) 1912
426) 50

427) Jack Warhop holds the Yankees' record for the most hit batsmen by a righthander in a season.

A) True
B) False

428) What is the Yankees' record for the most hit batsmen by a righthander in a season?

429) What year was this record set?

430) Who holds the Yankees' record for the most hit batsmen by a lefthander in a season?

431) What is the Yankees' record for the most hit batsmen by a lefthander in a season?

432) What year was this record set?

Answers:

427) A – True
428) 26
429) 1909
430) Tommy Byrne
431) 17
432) 1950

433) What is the Yankees' record for the most consecutive games hit safely right-handed?

434) Who holds the Yankees' record for the most consecutive games hit safely right-handed?

435) What year was this record set?

436) What is the record for the most consecutive games hit safely left-handed?

437) Who holds the Yankees' record for the most consecutive games hit safely left-handed?

438) The record for the most consecutive games hit safely left-handed was set in _____.

Answers:

433) 56; This is the MLB record.
434) Joe DiMaggio
435) 1941
436) 29
437) Earl Combs
438) 1931

439) Did Yankees pitcher Jack Chesbro ever complete 50 games in a season?

440) Is he ranked No. 1 on the Yankees' list for the most complete games in a season?

441) What year was the team's record set?

442) What is the next highest number of games that he completed in a season?

443) Was that good enough to capture the No. 2 spot on the Yankees' list for this category?

444) How many times does he appear on the Yankees' top 10 list for this category?

Answers:

439) No; The team record is 48.
440) Yes
441) 1904
442) 33
443) No; Jack Powell is No. 2 with 38, also in 1904.
444) Two; Nos. 1 and 5

☆ Progressive Trivia ☆

445) All time, how many American League Championships Series titles have the Yankees won?

446) How many of them have been in a sweep?

447) How many of their AL Championships concluded in New York?

448) How many times has New York been swept in an ALCS?

449) Who was the only team to sweep the Yankees in an ALCS?

450) All time, the Yankees have played in 20 ALCS.

    A) True
    B) False

Answers:

445) 11
446) One
447) Seven
448) Once
449) Kansas City Royals; 1980
450) B – False; The Yankees have played in 14 ALCS.

451) _____ holds the Yankees' career and single-season records for the most total bases.

452) How many total bases did he have in his career in New York?

453) His prowess at the plate earned him what nickname?

454) What season did he set the team record for the most total bases?

455) How many total bases did he have that season?

456) Who holds the Yankees' single-season record for the most total bases (right-handed)?

Answers:

451) Babe Ruth
452) 5,131
453) "The Sultan of Swat"
454) 1921
455) 457
456) Joe DiMaggio; 418 in 1937

☆ **Progressive Trivia** ☆

457) Elston Howard holds the Yankees' record for the highest fielding percentage by a catcher in a season.

    A) True
    B) False

458) What year was the Yankees' record set?

459) What is his record fielding percentage for the position?

460) How many total chances did he have that year?

461) How many games did he play in that season?

462) How old was he when he set this record?

Answers:

457) B – False; Yogi Berra holds this record.
458) 1958
459) 1.000
460) 550
461) 88; 88 at catcher, 132 total including 1B and outfield
462) 33

463) The Yankees' team record for the most runs by an opponent in a shutout game is _____.

464) What year was the team record set?

465) Which opponent scored the runs?

466) Where was the game played?

467) What is the team record for the most runs by opponents in a season?

468) What season did Yankees opponents set that mark?

Answers:

463) 22
464) 2004
465) Cleveland Indians
466) Yankee Stadium, Bronx, N.Y.
467) 898
468) 1930

469) Babe Ruth had 1,852 bases on balls in his career in New York.

   A) True
   B) False

470) What is his rank on the Yankees' career leaders list?

471) How many bases on balls did Mickey Mantle have in his career in New York?

472) He is ranked _____ of all time.

473) Who holds the No. 3 spot on the list?

474) With how many career bases on balls is he credited?

Answers:

469) A – True
470) No. 1
471) 1,733
472) No. 2
473) Lou Gehrig
474) 1,508

475) _____ owns the Yankees' career record for the most inside-the-park home runs.

476) How many inside-the-park home runs did he hit?

477) How many seasons did he play in New York?

478) Lou Gehrig is the only Yankee to have hit an inside-the-park home run in a World Series game.

    A) True
    B) False

479) How many inside-the-park home runs have opponents hit against the Yankees in World Series games?

480) Who was the most recent Yankee to hit an inside-the-park home run?

Answers:

475) Earle Combs
476) 23
477) 12
478) A – True
479) Two
480) Curtis Granderson; Aug. 21, 2011

481) Which Yankees right-handed pitcher maintained the
highest winning percentage for a season?

A) Alfredo Aceves
B) Aaron Small
C) Roger Clemens
D) Ron Davis

482) He set the Yankees' record in the category in _____.

483) What winning percentage did he earn that season?

484) What Yankees left-handed pitcher maintained the
highest winning percentage for a season?

485) What year did he set the record in the category?

486) What was his winning percentage that season?

Answers:

481) B – Aaron Small
482) 2005
483) 1.000; His record was 10-0.
484) Tom Zachary
485) 1929
486) 1.000; His record was 12-0.

487) What year did the Yankees play in their first-ever World Series?

488) Where was Game 1 of the series played?

489) Who was the Yankees' opponent in the series?

490) The series went to a decisive Game 8.

   A) True
   B) False

491) What was the final score of Game 8?

492) Was this the first World Series to be broadcast on radio?

Answers:

487) 1921
488) Polo Grounds in Manhattan, N.Y.
489) New York Giants
490) A – True; This was the last best-of-nine World Series.
491) Yankees 0, Giants 1
492) Yes

493) The Yankees' team record for the most times grounded into double play was set in _____.

494) How many double plays did Yankees batters ground into that season?

495) Paul O'Neill grounded into the most double plays that season.

A) True
B) False

496) How many double plays did he ground into?

497) Is this the most times he grounded into a double play in a season?

498) Which starting Yankees batter grounded into the fewest double plays during the record-setting season?

Answers:

493) 1996
494) 153
495) A – True
496) 21
497) No; 25 in 1995
498) Gerald Williams; Seven double plays

499) Who was the first-ever Yankees pitcher to win the AL Cy Young Award?

500) What year did he win the award?

501) Who was the most recent Yankees pitcher to win the award?

502) What year did he win the award?

503) How many times have Yankees pitchers won the coveted award?

504) How many major league pitchers have won the award more times individually than Yankees pitchers have won collectively?

Answers:

499) Bob Turley
500) 1958
501) Roger Clemens
502) 2001
503) Five
504) One; Roger Clemens, Seven times

505) Is the Yankees' team record for the most times caught stealing in a season more than 100?

506) How many games did they play that season?

507) The year was _____.

508) Is the Yankees' team record for the most stolen bases in a season more than 250?

509) How many games did they play that season?

510) The year was _____.

Answers:

505) No; 82
506) 154
507) 1920
508) Yes; 289
509) 156
510) 1910

511) What are the most .300 hitters the Yankees had in a season?

512) How many seasons have Yankees batters matched this team record?

513) What was the combined team batting average for those seasons?

514) How many of these .300 hitters were on each of these teams?

515) Did any Yankees batter with more than 200 at-bats in these seasons have a batting average above .400?

516) Did any Yankees batter with more than 200 at-bats in these seasons have a batting average under .300?

Answers:

511) Six
512) Three; 1930, 1931 and 1936
513) .302
514) Two; Lou Gehrig and Bill Dickey
515) No
516) Yes

517) Who was the Yankees' most recent American League MVP?

518) What year did he win the award?

519) Who was the Yankees' first-ever AL MVP?

520) What year did he win the award?

521) How many times has a Yankees player been named AL MVP?

522) How many Yankees have won the AL MVP on multiple occasions?

Answers:

517) Alex Rodriguez
518) 2007
519) Lou Gehrig
520) 1936
521) 19
522) Six

523) Who holds the Yankees' record for the most hits in a season?

    A) Don Mattingly
    B) Joe DiMaggio
    C) Alfonso Soriano
    D) Derek Jeter

524) He had _____ hits in the _____ season.

525) Who holds the record for the most hits in a season by a right-handed batter?

526) He had _____ hits in the _____ season.

527) Which Yankee holds the team record for the most hits by a switch hitter?

528) Which Yankee holds the team record for the most 200 hit seasons?

Answers:

523) A – Don Mattingly
524) 238, 1986
525) Derek Jeter
526) 219, 1999
527) Bernie Williams; 204 in 2002
528) Lou Gehrig; Eight seasons

529) What is the Yankees' record for the largest home crowd at a night game?

530) Who was the Yankees' opponent that night?

    A) Washington Senators
    B) Cleveland Indians
    C) St. Louis Browns
    D) Boston Red Sox

531) When was the game played?

532) Did the Yankees win the game?

533) What is the Yankees' record for the largest home crowd at a day game?

534) The game was played versus _____ in the _____ season.

Answers:

529) 74,747
530) D – Boston Red Sox
531) May 26, 1947
532) Yes
533) 74,200
534) Boston Red Sox, 1923: First opening day for Yankee Stadium.

535) Who holds the Yankees' career record for the most games played?

536) How many career games played does he have in New York?

537) How many career games started does he have?

538) Who is ranked No. 2 on the career list?

539) How many career games did he play with the Yankees?

540) He played for the Yankees from 1951-_____.

Answers:

535) Derek Jeter
536) 2,426
537) 1,908
538) Mickey Mantle
539) 2,401
540) 1968

☆ **Progressive Trivia** ☆

541) Who was the first-ever Yankees manager to be named the *Sporting News* Manager of the Year?

542) What year did he receive the award?

543) Did the Yankees win the World Series the year he received the honor?

544) Who was the most recent Yankees manager to be named the *Sporting News* Manager of the Year?

    A) Joe Torre
    B) Buck Showalter
    C) Bill Virdon
    D) Joe Girardi

545) What was the Yankees' regular-season record the year he received the honor?

546) All time, how many times have Yankees managers received the award?

Answers:

541) Joe McCarthy
542) 1936
543) Yes
544) A – Joe Torre
545) 114-48
546) 11; Seven different managers

Progressive Trivia

547) Have the Yankees claimed 50 all-time divisional titles?

548) How many of them are East Division titles?

549) What year was the baseball season split into two halves because of a strike?

550) Did the Yankees win the first half of the strike-shortened season?

551) What year did the Yankees win their most recent East Division title?

552) All time, how many Wild Card berths have the Yankees secured?

Answers:

547) No; 46
548) 18
549) 1981
550) Yes
551) 2011
552) Four

553) Alex Rodriguez was the last Yankee to successfully steal home.

A) True
B) False

554) When was the last time a Yankee stole home?

555) Was it a straight steal of home?

556) Against which team and catcher was the base stolen?

557) How many times did Babe Ruth steal home in his career?

558) Who is the Yankees career leader in this category?

Answers:

553) B – False; Brett Gardner
554) April 4, 2010
555) No; It was part of a double steal.
556) Boston Red Sox, Victor Martinez
557) 10
558) Lou Gehrig; 15

559) Was Mike Mussina the Yankees' most recent Rawlings
     Gold Glove winner?

560) In 2010, how many Yankees won a Rawlings Gold
     Glove Award.

561) Who has won the most Rawlings Gold Glove Awards
     as a Yankee?

562) All time, how many Yankees have won a Gold Glove
     Award?

563) Are Rawlings Gold Glove Winners selected by a panel
     of sportswriters and fans?

564) Bobby Shantz, the first Yankee to win a Gold Glove
     Award, played what position?

Answers:

559) No
560) Three; Mark Teixeira, Robinson Cano and Derek Jeter
561) Don Mattingly; Eight
562) 22
563) No; League managers and coaches
564) Pitcher

☆ **Progressive Trivia** ☆

565) Which legendary Yankee was nicknamed "Man Nobody Knows"?

566) Where was he born?

567) How many seasons did he play for New York?

568) How many career All-Star selections did he have?

569) What year was he inducted into the National Baseball Hall of Fame?

570) Jersey No. _____ was retired in his honor by the Yankees in 1972.

Answers:

565) Bill Dickey
566) Bastrop, La.
567) 19
568) 11
569) 1954
570) 8

☆ **Progressive Trivia** ☆

571) Have the Yankees ever played a game in which they scored at least one run in every inning?

572) Which season did the Yankees score the most runs per game?

573) Which season did the Yankees record the most hits per game?

574) Which season did The Yankees allow the most runs per game?

575) Which season did The Yankees allow the most hits per game?

576) When was the most recent season the Yankees allowed more runs than they scored?

    A) 1969
    B) 1988
    C) 1992
    D) 2008

Answers:

571) No
572) 1930; 6.9
573) 1930; 10.93
574) 1902; 6.01
575) 1902; 10.86
576) C – 1992

577) Who holds the Yankees' record for the most consecutive games won in a season by a righthander?

A) David Cone
B) Roger Clemens
C) Jack Chesbro
D) Red Ruffing

578) He set the record in _____.

579) How many consecutive games did he win that year?

580) How old was he that season?

581) What was his win-loss record that season?

582) How many games pitched did he record that year?

Answers:

577) B – Roger Clemens; Tied AL record
578) 2001
579) 16
580) 38
581) 20-3
582) 33

583) Casey Stengel was named manager of the New York Yankees in 1949.

    A) True
    B) False

584) How many seasons did Stengel spend as the Yankees' skipper?

585) During his MLB playing career Stengel played for ___ MLB teams.

586) He was a player for which MLB teams?

587) What position did Stengel play during his MLB career?

588) He played against the Yankees in the 1923 World Series, where he was the first to do what?

Answers:

583) A – True
584) 12
585) Five
586) Brooklyn Dodgers, Pittsburgh Pirates, Philadelphia Phillies, New York Giants and Boston Braves
587) Outfield
588) Hit a World Series home run in Yankee Stadium

589) What year were the first-ever Silver Slugger Awards given?

590) How many Yankees received a Silver Slugger Award that year?

591) The Yankees team record for the most players receiving a Silver Slugger Award in the same season was in 1980.

   A) True
   B) False

592) Who was the most recent Yankees to win a Silver Slugger Award?

593) They received the honor in _____.

594) All time, how many Yankees have been honored with Silver Slugger Awards?

Answers:

589) 1980
590) Two
591) B – False; Four in 1985 and 2002
592) Robinson Cano and Curtis Granderson
593) 2011
594) 37

595) Which Yankees batter had the most hits in 2011?

596) How many hits did he have?

597) Which Yankee had the second most hits in 2011?

598) How many hits did he have?

599) _____ had the third most hits in 2011.

600) How many hits did he have?

Answers:

595) Robinson Cano
596) 188
597) Derek Jeter
598) 162
599) Curtis Granderson
600) 153

601) Which team is a party to the Yankees' team record for the most combined hits in a game?

    A) Detroit Tigers
    B) Tampa Bay Rays
    C) Chicago White Sox
    D) Toronto Blue Jays

602) What year did the teams combine to set this record?

603) How many combined hits did they have?

604) The game was played at _____.

605) Did the teams also combine for greater than 25 runs?

606) Who left the field with a victory that day?

Answers:

601) A – Detroit Tigers
602) 1928
603) 45; Tied AL record
604) Navin Field, Detroit, Mich.
605) Yes
606) Detroit; Yankees 10, Tigers 19

607) Since 1970, what is the Yankees' team record for the longest winning streak?

    A) 9 games
    B) 11 games
    C) 12 games
    D) 14 games

608) When was this mark set?

609) Which opponent ended the streak?

610) The Yankees' all-time longest winning streak took place in _____.

611) How many games comprised that streak?

612) Against which team did that streak begin?

Answers:

607) B – 11 games
608) 1985
609) Milwaukee Brewers
610) 1947
611) 19
612) Washington Senators

613) The Yankees' team record for the most hits in a season is _____.

614) How many games did the team play that season?

615) What year was the record set?

    A) 1930
    B) 1936
    C) 1950
    D) 1998

616) What Yankees batter led the team in hits that year?

617) How many hits did he have?

618) Did he play in all of the team's games that year?

Answers:

613) 1,683
614) 154
615) A – 1930
616) Lou Gehrig
617) 220
618) Yes

619) Has a Yankees pitcher ever struck out four batters in one inning?

620) _____ is the pitcher who accomplished the feat.

621) What year did he record the rare feat?

622) What team was New York facing that day?

623) In which inning did the four strikeouts occur?

624) How many total strikeouts did he record that game?

Answers:

619) Yes
620) A. J. Burnett
621) 2011
622) Colorado Rockies
623) Sixth
624) Five

625) What university did Roger Clemens attend?

    A) Oklahoma
    B) Florida State
    C) UCLA
    D) Texas

626) Joba Chamberlain attended Nebraska.

    A) True
    B) False

627) Did Brett Gardner go to Clemson?

628) Curtis Granderson played outfield for the _____.

629) Where did Jorge Posada play his college baseball?

630) Was Mark Teixeira a Georgia Tech Yellow Jacket or
      LSU Tiger?

Answers:

625) D – Texas
626) A – True; Nebraska-Kearney then Nebraska-Lincoln
627) No; He attended College of Charleston.
628) Illinois; Illini
629) Calhoun Community College
630) Georgia Tech Yellow Jacket

631) Which Yankee hit the first-ever home run in All-Star Game history?

632) How many total home runs did he hit in his All-Star Game appearances?

633) Who was the most recent Yankee to hit a homer in the Midsummer Classic?

A) Alfonso Soriano
B) Jason Giambi
C) Yogi Berra
D) Derek Jeter

634) How many times has a Yankee won the Home Run Derby at the All-Star Game?

635) Who was the most recent Yankee to win the Home Run Derby?

636) All time, how many home runs have Yankees players hit in the Home Run Derby?

Answers:

631) Babe Ruth
632) One
633) B – Jason Giambi
634) Three
635) Robinson Cano
636) 99; The Yankees lead all other teams, Seattle is next with 77.

637) Who did the Yankees play in the 2000 World Series?

638) Who was the home team for the series?

639) Game 5's attendance exceeded 50,000.

    A) True
    B) False

640) How many games did Andy Pettitte pitch in the series?

641) What was Pettitte's series ERA?

642) Who was named the Most Valuable Player of that year's World Series?

Answers:

637) New York Mets
638) New York Yankees
639) A – True; 55,292 at Shea Stadium
640) Two
641) 1.98
642) Derek Jeter

643) What year was the Yankee's team award known as the James P. Dawson Award established?

644) Who was James P. Dawson?

645) Recipients of the award are selected by a vote of

_____.

646) The award is given to the most outstanding rookie in Spring Training.

A) True
B) False

647) Who was the first recipient of the James P. Dawson Award?

648) Who was the most recent recipient of the James P. Dawson Award?

Answers:

643) 1956
644) A long-time *New York Times* sportswriter
645) New York Yankees beat writers
646) A – True
647) Norm Siebern
648) Manny Banuelos

649) What is the Yankees' record for the lowest ERA in a career?

650) Which Yankee set this team record?

651) How many seasons did he spend in New York?

652) _____ was his last season in the New York.

653) How many Earned Runs did he allow in his career with the Yankees?

654) Who holds the No. 2 spot on the Yankees' career list for the lowest ERA?

    A) Al Orth
    B) Sparky Lyle
    C) Mariano Rivera
    D) Russ Ford

Answers:

649) 2.14
650) Rich Gossage
651) Seven
652) 1989
653) 127
654) C – Mariano Rivera

655) What is the record attendance for a game at Yankee Stadium III?

656) Was this set during a regular-season or postseason game?

657) This record was set in _____.

658) Who was the Yankees' opponent that game?

659) Was the record crowd treated to a Yankees victory?

660) What was the contest's final score?

Answers:

655) 50,960
656) Postseason game; ALDS game five
657) 2011
658) Detroit Tigers
659) No
660) Tigers 3, Yankees 2

661) Legendary Yankees sportscaster Mel Allen was born in Mobile, Ala.

    A) True
    B) False

662) Where did Mel attend university?

663) What year did Mel broadcast his first-ever Yankees baseball game?

664) Was "How a-bout that?!" one of Mel's catchphrases?

665) How many World Series' did Mel call during his career?

666) During which World Series did Mel lose his voice?

Answers:

661) B – False; Birmingham, Ala.
662) Alabama; Crimson Tide
663) 1939
664) Yes
665) 22
666) 1963

667) Did the Yankees' ever have a costumed mascot?

668) The Yankees introduced the mascot in _____.

669) What was the nickname of the mascot?

670) He was a large pinstriped bird with a mustache that made him resemble which former Yankee great?

671) How many years was he the Yankees mascot?

672) While playing outfield for the Yankees, Lou Piniella once chased and threw his glove at the San Diego Chicken.

   A) True
   B) False

Answers:

667) Yes
668) 1979
669) Dandy
670) Thurman Munson
671) Three
672) A – True

673) During Spring Training, are the Yankees members of the Cactus or Grapefruit League?

674) In what city can they be found?

675) Yankees Spring Training was first held there in _____.

676) What is the name of the Yankees home field during Spring Training?

677) What is the seating capacity of the Yankees spring training home field?

678) Who is famously quoted as saying, "These days baseball is different. You come to spring training, you get your legs ready, you arms loose, your agents ready and your lawyer lined up"?

Answers:

673) Grapefruit League
674) Tampa, Fla.
675) 1996
676) George M Steinbrenner Field
677) 11,076
678) Dave Winfield

679) In 2011, the Yankees became the first team in history to hit three grand slams in a game, which player did not hit a grand slam in the game?

A) Robinson Cano
B) Curtis Granderson
C) Derek Jeter
D) Russell Martin

680) Against which team did the Yankees hit the three grand slams?

681) What was the final score of the game?

682) Which Yankee holds the record for most grand slams in a career?

683) How many did he hit?

684) Which Yankee pitcher hit an inside-the-park grand slam in 1964?

Answers:

679) C – Derek Jeter
680) Oakland Athletics
681) Yankees 22, Athletics 9
682) Lou Gehrig
683) 23
684) Mel Stottlemyre

685) Whitey Ford holds the Yankees' career record for the most wins.

    A) True
    B) False

686) How many career wins does the career leader have?

687) _____ sits in the No. 2 spot on the Yankees' career list for the most wins.

688) How many wins did he have?

689) Is Andy Pettitte ranked in the top five on this list?

690) How many career wins does he have?

Answers:

685) A – True
686) 236
687) Red Ruffing
688) 231
689) Yes; No. 3
690) 203

691) When Babe Ruth retired with 714 home runs, who was the only other player to have more than 300 home runs?

692) Who hit the first-ever home run in the original Yankee Stadium?

693) Who holds the record for most home runs hit at Yankee Stadium?

694) Who hit the second most home runs at Yankee Stadium?

695) Who holds the No. 3 spot on the list for most home runs in Yankee Stadium?

696) Which Yankee was the first in the AL to hit four home runs in the same game?

Answers:

691) Lou Gehrig; 378 at that time
692) Babe Ruth; April 18, 1923
693) Mickey Mantle; 266
694) Babe Ruth; 259
695) Lou Gehrig; 251
696) Lou Gehrig; June 3, 1932

697) Has any Yankees player ever homered on his first MLB at-bat?

698) How many Yankees players have accomplished this feat?

699) Who was the first-ever Yankee player to do it?

700) Who was the most recent Yankee to hit a home run in his first MLB at-bat?

701) What year did he do it?

    A) 2002
    B) 2004
    C) 2005
    D) 2007

702) Against which team did he do it?

Answers:

697) Yes
698) Three
699) John Miller
700) Andy Phillips
701) B – 2004
702) Boston Red Sox

703) Who was the first Yankee to be honored with a monument in the outfield?

704) What year was this monument placed in Yankee Stadium?

705) How many total monuments on large red granite blocks are in Monument Park?

706) The original Monument Park at Yankee Stadium I was in play in the outfield.

    A) True
    B) False

707) How many total plaques are in Monument Park?

708) How many former Yankee owners are honored with a plaque?

Answers:

703) Miller Huggins; Manager
704) 1932
705) Five; Miller Huggins, Lou Gehrig, Babe Ruth, Mickey Mantle and Joe DiMaggio
706) A – True
707) 27
708) Two; Jack Ruppert and George Steinbrenner

709) When was the last time Yankees batters hit three consecutive home runs?

710) The consecutive home runs were hit off a Boston Red Sox pitcher?

    A) True
    B) False

711) Who hit the first of the three home runs?

712) Who hit the second of the three home runs?

713) Who hit the third and final home run of the three?

714) The only other time the Yankees accomplished this feat was five _____ earlier?

Answers:

709) June 3, 1984
710) B – False; Toronto Blue Jays
711) Oscar Gamble
712) Steve Kemp
713) Toby Harrah
714) Days

715) Who played the most full seasons as a Yankee?

716) _____ players have played 18 seasons in New York.

717) Does Mickey Mantle also own the record for the most All-Star game selections as a Yankee?

718) Who has the second most All-Star game selections for New York?

719) What is Lou Gehrig's career record for the most consecutive games played for New York?

720) Joe McCarthy has the distinction of managing the Yankees for the most years, most games, most wins and most losses.

    A) True
    B) False

Answers:

715) Mickey Mantle
716) Two; Mickey Mantle and Yogi Berra
717) Yes
718) Yogi Berra
719) 2,130
720) A – True; 16 years, 2,348 games, 1,460 wins and 867 losses

All information in this book is valid
as of the end of the
2011 season.